The French

Casey Horton

CRABTREE
Publishing Company

CRABTREE
Publishing Company

PMB 16A, 350 Fifth Avenue
Suite 3308
New York, NY 10118

612 Welland Avenue
St. Catharines, Ontario,
Canada L2M 5V6

Co-ordinating editor: Ellen Rodger
Content editor: Virginia Mainprize
Production co-ordinator: Rosie Gowsell
Cover design: Robert MacGregor

Film: Embassy Graphics

Printer

Worzalla Publishing Company

Created by:
Brown Partworks Ltd
Commissioning editor: Anne O'Daly
Project editor: Caroline Beattie
Picture researcher: Adrian Bentley
Editorial assistant: Chris Wiegand
Maps: Mark Walker
Consultant: Donald Avery, Ph.D

CATALOGING-IN-PUBLICATION DATA
Horton, Casey.
    The French / Casey Horton.–1st ed.
        p.cm. – (We Came to North America)
    Includes index.
    Summary: Examines the history, traditions and
contributions of French settlers who came to the New
World.
    ISBN 0-7787-0199-9 (pbk.) – ISBN 0-7787-0185-9 (rlb).
    1.French Americans–History–Juvenile literature.2.
French Americans–Biography–Juvenile literature. 3.
Pioneers–United States–History-Juvenile literature.4.
Pioneers–United States–Biography–Juvenile literature. 5.
Frontier and pioneer life–United States–Juvenile
literature. [1. French Americans. 2. Pioneers. 3. Frontier
and pioneer life.] I.Title. II. Series.
    E184.F8 H67 2000
    973'.0441–dc21   LC 00-049114
                              CIP

Photographs

AKG London Uffizi Gallery, Florence 4; **The Art
Archive** 25 (bottom); New York Public Library 8;
Corbis Archivo Iconografico 21 (bottom); Austrian
Archives 18 (top); Earl Kowall 27 (bottom); Mark
Gibson 23 (bottom); Owen Franken front cover, 29
(top); Paul A. Souders 5 (top); Philip Gould 23 (top);
Richard T. Nowitz 24; Robert Holmes 10 (top), 14, 15
(top). David Noble 29 (bottom); EMPICS John Marsh
30 (bottom).**Genesis Space Photo Library** NASA
31 (bottom); Hulton Getty 30 (top); Mark Borkowski
Press & PR Al Seib 31 (top); Mary Evans Picture
Library title page, 9 (top); **Metropolitan Toronto
Reference Library** 26; (JRR 2059) 15 (bottom);
National Archives of Canada (C-11226) 6, (C-
1026) 10 (bottom), (C-139973) 17, (C-57) 21(top).
National Gallery of Canada ("A View of Chateau
Richer, Cape Torment and the lower end of the Isle
of Orleans near Quebec" by Thomas Davies. Acc. no.
6275) 20; ("Leeward of the Island (1.47)" by Paul-
Emile Borduas. Acc. no. 6098. © The Estate of
Paul-Emile Borduas) 27 (top); **North Wind Picture
Archives** 18 (bottom), 19. **Peter Newark's Pictures**
7, 9 (bottom), 11, 13, 22, 25 (top), back cover.
Sylvia Pitcher 28; **Travel Ink** Mark Summerfield 5
(bottom).

Cover

Cajun Chef Paul Prudhomme in New Orleans,
with a skillet of jambalaya, a stew of meat,
vegetables, and rice.

Book credits

Page 12: *The Romance of Canada: Stories from
the History of Her Discovery, Exploration,
Conquest & Settlement*, Herbert Strang, ed.,
Henry Frowde and Hodder and Stoughton,
London.
Page 16: *New England and New France:
Contrasts and Parallels in Colonial History*,
James Douglas LLD, G.P. Putnam's and Sons,
New York and London (1913).

Contents

Introduction

The French made their first voyages to North America 450 years ago. For the next 150 years, they built settlements in what is today eastern Canada. They also explored to the west and south, deep into the heart of the continent.

For hundreds of years before that, traders and merchants had traveled overland across Europe to Asia. They **imported** silks and spices, tapestries, and porcelain, which were not available in Europe. In time, some of the new empires that lay along the trade routes to Asia did not want **foreigners** crossing their territory. A new sea route had to be found. Because Europeans did not know of the existence of the Americas, some explorers believed they would find a short way to Asia by sailing west across the Atlantic.

The first French people who came to North America were explorers, sent by the French king to search for a shorter route to Asia and to find a land of great wealth. They claimed the land for France, but they found neither the Northwest Passage, the **fabled** short water route to the Far East, nor gold and precious metals. They did, however, find beaver pelts and other furs that could be sold for large sums of money in Europe.

The French did not settle the colony for almost another hundred years. At first, they built bases for fur traders. These forts were also used by French priests who traveled to native villages, hoping to **convert** the Native Americans to **Christianity**.

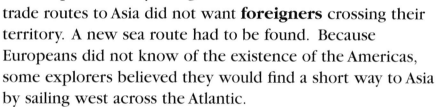

▲ In 1713, the French territories covered a large area of North America and half of the island of Hispaniola, now called Haiti.

◀ Francis I was a French king who encouraged explorers to go to North America to look for riches.

Signposts

The maps of the United States and Canada are dotted with French names that mark the places where the French explored or settled long ago. All over North America, there are thousands of French names, such as Baton Rouge (red stick), Lachine (China), Belle Isle (beautiful island), and Terre Haute (high land). La Crosse, a town and river in Wisconsin, was named after the French word for the Native-American game played with a netted stick and a ball. The French thought the stick looked like a crosier — a bishop's stick or staff, which is called *la crosse* in French.

▲ **La crosse is a fast game played both professionally and in some schools.**

Gradually, more French people came to New France and settled along the St. Lawrence River, on the Atlantic coast of Canada, and as far south as Louisiana. Some were farmers, coming to make a home with their families. Others were artisans: carpenters, metalworkers, and stone masons, who practiced their craft in the towns. Soldiers were sent from France to defend the **colony** from attack, and government officials came to rule this vast territory in the name of the king. Life was often hard. The climate was harsh and supplies were scarce. Sometimes, homes and villages were attacked by the Iroquois, who were at war with the Hurons, the allies of the French.

▼ This church in South Carolina was built by French Protestants whose ancestors settled there in the 1600s.

Eventually, because of wars in Europe, France lost all its colonies in North America to England and Spain. The colonists, however, stayed, and French-speaking people still live in many of the areas their **ancestors** settled hundreds of years ago. Even in areas of the United States where French is no longer spoken, the original French names of towns and places have been kept, a reminder of the days when these areas were explored and settled by the French. The French language, music, culture, and *joie de vivre*, or joy of living, survived and have, over the centuries, enriched so much of North American life.

Cartier's Gold

The first European explorers to reach North America were Spanish and English. They came looking for a sea route to Asia. Instead, they found land. Having no idea how large the continent was, they continued to search for a Northwest Passage to Asia.

After England and Spain claimed sections of North America as their own, France decided it too wanted a share of these lands. In 1534, King Francis I of France sent Jacques Cartier, a sea captain from the north of France, to "discover...islands and countries...where...he should find great quantities of gold and other valuable things."

After crossing the Atlantic Ocean for twenty days, Cartier's two little ships traveled up the gulf of a huge river and, on July 16, landed on the shore of the Gaspé Peninsula. Cartier put up a 30-foot (10-meter) wooden cross and claimed the land for France.

A group of Iroquois paddled out in their canoes to greet these strange men in their sailing ships. Cartier offered them knives, hatchets, and glass beads, and was given furs in exchange. He persuaded the chief to allow two of his sons to sail back to France with him and promised that they would all return soon.

Cartier's voyage was a failure because he found neither gold nor a passage to Asia. However, the king was impressed with the stories the chief's sons told of a land of great wealth beyond the lands Cartier had seen. Francis I commissioned a second voyage. The next year, Cartier again set sail, this time with 3 ships and 110 men.

On this voyage, the Iroquois showed him the mouth of the St. Lawrence River. Cartier traveled up the river to Stadacona, the site of present-day Québec City, where the Iroquois were returned to their father, chief Donnacona.

▲ Cartier was the first explorer to write about the area around the St. Lawrence River and Newfoundland.

Cartier and Donnacona

After their terrible winter of cold and sickness, Cartier and his men were invited to a good-bye feast by the Iroquois. Cartier convinced the chief, Donnacona, to return to France with him and promised to bring him back on his next voyage. Chief Donnacona told the king wonderful stories of fabulous treasure and even one-legged men who lived without eating. Despite Cartier's promise, Donnacona never returned home. He died in France before Cartier's final voyage in 1541.

◄ A map drawn in France in 1546 showing Jacques Cartier and his party in New France, surrounded by Native Americans.

After exploring up and down the river, Cartier decided to spend the winter in Stadacona. He was not prepared for the bitter cold and scurvy, a terrible disease which struck nearly a hundred of his men and killed twenty-five. Had the Iroquois not shown him how to make a medicine of cedar bark, many more would have died. When spring finally came, the river ice melted, and Cartier sailed for France.

It took five years for Cartier to convince Francis I to pay for another voyage to North America. This time, Cartier and his men collected twelve barrels of gold and diamonds before returning home. The gold turned out to be worthless iron pyrites, and the diamonds were nothing but crystals.

Cartier's voyages ended in failure. France lost interest in the new colony. Sixty-seven years later, the French population of Québec still numbered only 22 people.

▲ Jacques Cartier's journeys exploring what is now Canada. He and his men were the first Europeans to travel so far inland.

New France

For over 60 years after the first French explorers arrived in New France and claimed the territory for the French king, the colony was abandoned. Wars with other European countries kept the French busy at home. The only contact was made by fishing boats, sailing to catch cod in the waters off Newfoundland and Nova Scotia.

By the beginning of the 1600s, France was entering a period of peace. This fact, and the growing market for furs from North America, sparked a new interest in New France.

The king granted Sieur de Monts and Samuel de Champlain, an explorer who had already traveled up the St. Lawrence, a ten-year **monopoly** on the fur trade in New France. In 1605, de Monts and Champlain, wanting to establish a base for the trade, chose a site on the Bay of Fundy coast of what is today Nova Scotia. The settlement was called Port Royal and was the capital of Acadia, the first colony in New France.

▲ A map showing the people, animals, and plants that the French found in North America.

The Order of Good Cheer

To keep up the **morale** of his men, especially during the long, cold winter, Champlain established the Order of Good Cheer. Every two weeks, one of the men was to act as host for an evening of good food and entertainment. He was responsible for catching and cooking the food for the party and for organizing music and skits to amuse the others. Everyone looked forward to the evenings, and because of them, the men remained healthy and in good spirits.

▶ **Members of the Order of Good Cheer walk through the streets of Port Royal.**

The colonists built a two-story, wooden fort with a courtyard in the middle. They knew they could not rely on ships from France to bring supplies through the harsh winter, so they planted wheat and vegetables outside the fort. Even though they established friendly relations with the neighboring Micmacs, the colony did not prosper. In 1607, it was abandoned.

The next year, Champlain and a group of fur traders, priests, and soldiers traveled up the St. Lawrence River and built a fort at Québec. It was a fur trading post where the natives came and traded furs in exchange for guns, blankets, and cooking utensils. The fort became a small colony when the first settlers arrived in 1617, but it grew slowly at first. Fifteen years after it had been founded, there were only fourteen permanent settlers and five children in Québec. Today, Québec is a large, thriving city and the capital of the province of Québec, and Champlain is known as the father of New France.

▲ **The explorer Samuel de Champlain founded a French settlement at Québec, on the St. Lawrence River.**

The Fur Trade

The first French to settle in New France came for one reason: fur. In fact, some historians say that the fur trade led to the establishment of New France.

In the late 1500s, men's hats, made from beaver fur, became the fashion rage of Europe. The first fur traders were French fishers, visiting the fishing grounds around Newfoundland and Nova Scotia. They met Native Americans and exchanged cloth, pots and pans, guns, and knives for beaver pelts. Realizing the huge profits that could be made, more and more traders came to New France. The trade grew rapidly and eventually centered at the settlement at Montréal, up the river from Québec.

In 1628, the French king granted **exclusive** fur trading rights to a group of French merchants known as the Company of One Hundred Associates. In return, the company promised to encourage **emigration** from France to the colony and raise the population to 4000 in fifteen years. It also agreed to help Roman Catholic priests convert the Native Americans.

There were many men in New France who traded and sold furs illegally. Some traveled back and forth across the Atlantic and had no intention of settling in the new colony. Others were colonists who quickly discovered that clearing the land was hard work. They left their farms to trap beaver or to travel west into the interior and trade for furs.

▲ **Hats made of beaver pelts were so popular that the European beaver was near extinction because of overhunting. French merchants became enormously wealthy importing beaver pelts from New France.**

◄ **The French *coureurs de bois* traveled to Native American villages to trade French guns, blankets, and other goods in exchange for North American furs.**

Trading Missions

French fur traders traveled to Native American settlements on trading **treks** using canoes for transportation on rivers and lakes. They were sometimes joined by Roman Catholic priests. The French traders formed alliances with some Native Americans but not with others. The Hurons, whom the French supported, were at war with the Iroquois, and that war spread to include the French. At times of conflict, the Huron brought their beaver pelts down river to the French post at Montréal. In spring, when their birch bark canoes arrived filled with furs, there was a great celebration with speeches, food, and music.

▶ A *coureur de bois* carried few things with him on his journey into the forest.

These fur traders were known as *coureurs de bois*, or runners of the woods. They were often the first Europeans to explore and map large areas of North America. Soon, there were so many illegal fur traders that officials tried to stop them from leaving their farms. Only men with permits could trade, and anyone who traded without a permit was threatened with fines or **excommunication** from the Church. The rule was impossible to enforce in such a large and unsettled area. The *coureurs de bois* made friends with Native Americans, especially the Huron and Algonquin. The traders adopted many Native American ways and learned Native American skills, such as hunting, trapping, canoeing, and using local plants and berries as food and medicine. Some *coureurs de bois* married Native American women. The children of these unions were known as Métis.

As the supply of beaver pelts from the St. Lawrence and Great Lakes regions decreased, fur traders traveled further west, north, and south. They established forts along the Ohio River valley, Hudson Bay, and founded a colony as far south as Louisiana.

▼ French explorers traveled inland into North America in the late seventeenth and early eighteenth centuries.

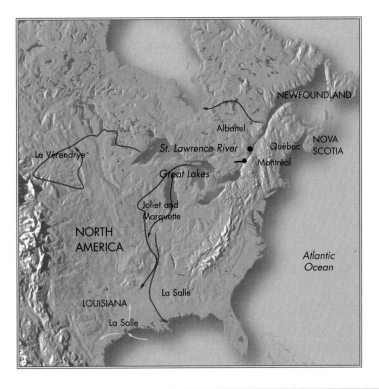

NEWFOUNDLAND

Albanel

St. Lawrence River • Québec

NOVA SCOTIA

La Vérendrye

Montréal

Great Lakes

Joliet and Marquette

NORTH AMERICA

Atlantic Ocean

LOUISIANA

La Salle

La Salle

Eyewitness to History

PIERRE ESPRIT RADISSON was a *coureur de bois* and explorer who came to New France at the age of seventeen. He was taken prisoner by the Iroquois and lived with them for two years.

"

The next day we marched into a village, where we were greeted with loud outcries from all sides. Our party sat down, and I in the middle of them; and very soon I saw advancing towards us a number of Indians, armed with staves, and evidently bent on doing mischief. They stripped me of my clothes, but before they could do me any injury I was rescued by a kind old woman, who had come near me, accompanied by a boy carrying a hatchet. The woman gave me back some of my clothes, while the young man took me by the hand and led me safely out of the company. They brought me to their hut, where they treated me with great kindness.

   I was now parted from the Indians who had taken me captive in the first place, and continued to dwell in this village, where, after some time I formed many acquaintances. I did all I could to make myself familiar with their ways. During the time I stayed with these people I suffered no wrong at their hands, and was allowed entire freedom of movement. Of this privilege I fully availed myself. I had a small gun at my command, and took all the pleasure imaginable in shooting partridges and squirrels, and joining in the games of my companions. I frequently had presents made to me by one or another, all of which I handed over to the old woman with whom I dwelt for safe keeping. She called me by the name of her son (who had before been killed) Orinha — a word which signifies stone.

"

Priests and Missions

In France, many people saw New France as a land where Native Americans had to be converted to Christianity. French priests traveled across the Atlantic and into the interior of Canada to live among and preach to the Native Americans.

◀ Ste. Marie among the Hurons was a Jesuit mission and Ontario's first European settlement. It has been reconstructed to show what life was like in the settlement in the seventeenth century.

The first priests to come to New France were **missionaries** who lived with Native Americans. Their lives were hard and often dangerous and very different from the lives they had led in France. They hoped to teach Native American tribes about Christianity, which they believed was the only true religion. The Native Americans had their own spiritual traditions and often resented the priests, whom they called "black robes." Some of the priests were killed in wars between native tribes. Others were captured, tortured, and killed by the Iroquois, the enemies of the French.

In 1638, a group of priests established a mission, called Ste. Marie among the Hurons, on Georgian Bay, over 650 miles (1000 kilometers) from the permanent French settlements along the St. Lawrence. Over time, the mission grew to include a **chapel**, barns, a cook house, a hospital, a blacksmith's shop, and homes for the priests, lay workers, and Native Americans living in the mission.

Religious Schools

Priests and nuns were important in the life of New France. They built schools where both French and Native-American children learned to read and write. Nuns taught young girls, both French and Native-American, reading, writing, singing, and needlework. A seminary to train priests was built in Québec. In both Québec and Montréal, nuns opened hospitals to look after the sick and elderly.

◄ **This convent, a building where nuns live and train, stands in the French quarter of New Orleans, Louisiana.**

Some Hurons converted to Christianity, sometimes because they believed what the missionaries taught, or because they were rewarded with gifts and tobacco. Others deeply resented the influence of the missionaries, especially after a deadly **epidemic** of measles and smallpox attacked the Huron. In 1648, because of the threat of attack from the Iroquois, enemies of the Huron, the priests burned Ste. Marie among the Hurons to the ground.

▼ **The Jesuits in New France were a powerful group. Their properties included the Jesuit church and college in Québec, shown here in the eighteenth century.**

A lot is known about the work of the priests who went to live among Native Americans and hoped to convert them to Christianity. The missionaries belonged to an order of priests known as the Jesuits. Each priest kept a detailed account of his work in New France which was sent to the Jesuit office in France. These documents, known as the Jesuit Relations, tell us a great deal about life in New France.

Eyewitness to History

The Ursulines were the first nuns to come to New France. MARIE DE L'INCARNATION was the superior of the Ursulines. She recorded some of her experiences teaching girls in the convent at Québec. In 1661, she wrote:

" Some pupils remain six or seven years, others in the short space of twelve months must be taught their prayers, reading, writing, and arithmetic, and the Church's doctrines and morals — in short, all that is most essential in the education of females.

To begin with, we have permanently seven nuns engaged in the instruction of French girls, in addition to two lay sisters engaged in outside work. The Indian girls are lodged and boarded with the French, but to instruct them we need one special teacher, and sometimes more, when their number increases. Just now, to my extreme regret, I must refuse admission to seven Algonquin scholars because we could not provide them with even food. Ever since our arrival in Canada, despite our poverty, we have not turned any from our door, and therefore the necessity which now obliges us to reject these girls causes me sincere sorrow, but we must admit to an exigency, so exacting that we have been obliged to send some of our French girls back to their parents. We have had to restrict our scholars to the twelve French and three Indians, two of whom are Iroquois, one of them a captive, to whom we are requested to endeavor to teach French.

In this country, great pains are taken to educate the French girls, and I can assure you that but for the care exerted by the Ursulines, their salvation would be in constant danger.

The Colony Grows

Although the Company of One Hundred Associates had promised to send settlers, the colony grew slowly. In 1663, the French population was still only a few thousand, most of whom were men. Many were soldiers, sent by the king to defend the colony against the English, who controlled the areas to the south, and their allies the Iroquois.

In 1663, the French king Louis XIV ended the Company of One Hundred Associates' monopoly in New France and made it a royal colony under his direct control. He appointed three men to govern New France. The governor ruled the colony and controlled the army. The bishop looked after the schools, hospitals, and the work of the missionaries and priests. The intendant was in charge of the courts, the fur trade, and the finances. The new intendant was eager to bring much-needed settlers. Young men from France were encouraged to come and work as hired men, or *engagés*. They received free passage on a ship to New France, room and board, and a small wage. Young peasant farmers, attracted by the promise of free land and excellent hunting and fishing, also came to make a new home for themselves.

▲ An astrolabe was used to help people to calculate their position at sea as well as on land.

◄ The *filles du roi* traveled across the Atlantic to marry and raise families.

The Journey

The journey across the ocean was often very difficult. The crossing from France to Québec could take as long as ten to twelve weeks. Heavy storms tossed the ships about on the waves, and many of the ships were in dangerously poor condition. Many ships carried more people than was legally allowed. Passengers had to bring their own food and were crowded together in the dark and unhealthy living area below the deck.

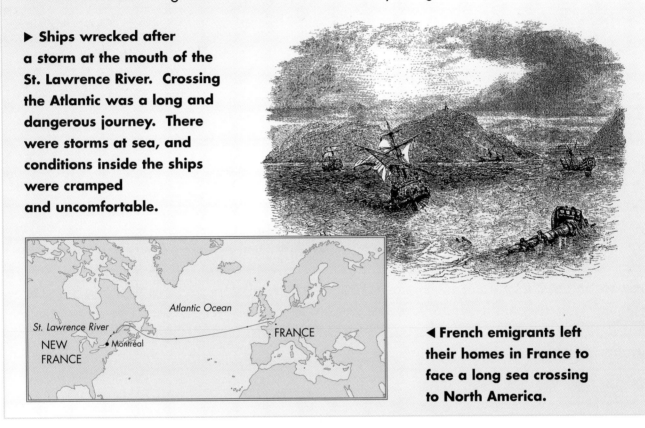

▶ **Ships wrecked after a storm at the mouth of the St. Lawrence River. Crossing the Atlantic was a long and dangerous journey. There were storms at sea, and conditions inside the ships were cramped and uncomfortable.**

Atlantic Ocean

St. Lawrence River

NEW FRANCE

• Montréal

• FRANCE

◀ **French emigrants left their homes in France to face a long sea crossing to North America.**

To solve the problem of so many single French men in the colony, the king ordered that young, healthy, unmarried French women of good character be transported to New France. These women were known as the *filles du roi,* or daughters of the king. They were given a free trip to New France and a **dowry** directly from the king. Each was given one ox, one cow, two pigs, two chickens, and two barrels of salt pork.

In the next ten years, 774 French women arrived in New France. Large families were encouraged, and families with ten or more living children were given a yearly pension. Single French men who did not marry within fifteen days after the arrival of a shipload of *filles du roi* were not granted a permit for fur trading. The French population grew rapidly, and by 1675, there were 8000 French people living in the colony.

Life in New France

Although Native Americans had lived, hunted, and traded in these lands for thousands of years, the king claimed all the territory in New France as his own. He gave large areas of land along the rivers to important people, called *seigneurs*.

The *seigneur* divided his land into long strips, called *rotures*, running up from the river to the forest wilderness. Each lot was given to a farming family. The tenant farmer, or *habitant*, had to build a house, **cultivate** his land, pay taxes to the *seigneur*, and work on the *seigneur's* land for three or four days a year. The seigneur was responsible for building a house and mill on his own land, for paying part of the cost of building a church, and for helping with the construction of bridges and roads.

The first job of the *habitant* was to clear the land, chopping trees and burning stumps. Because families ate so much bread, one of the most important crops was wheat. Farmers also grew hay for their animals and kept a vegetable garden. They raised chickens and pigs for meat, cows for milk and meat, and horses to pull their plows and sleighs.

▼ Farms in New France were long strips that ran from the forest to the river, so that each farming family could reach and use both.

▲ A group of habitants at home. Some are playing cards, one is holding a baby, and another is warming herself by the stove.

Life at first was hard for *habitant* families, but it was often better than the lives they had lived in France. They owned their own farms, there was free wood for building and heating, and the forests and rivers were filled with wild animals and fish.

Habitants built their houses using logs, excellent **insulators** against the wind and cold. Roofs were steeply sloped so the snow would slide off easily. A huge fireplace in the kitchen-living room was used for both cooking and heating. Chairs, a table, a bench-bed, and cots for the children were made by the *habitants* during the long winters and were painted bright red. Hand-hooked rugs made the room cosy and comfortable.

The long winters were a time for sleighing and skating on the frozen river and for having parties. The whole family bundled up and set off in their sleigh over the snow to visit friends or relatives. Weddings and **baptisms,** were important events with lots of food, and singing and dancing that lasted well into the night.

Tinker, Tailor, Soldier...

Not everyone in New France was a farmer or a fur trader. Many people lived in the towns and worked as carpenters, shopkeepers, stonemasons, and artisans. Others were priests, doctors, and teachers. Québec was the largest town in New France. The wealthiest and most important people lived in comfortable stone houses in the upper town. Below, near the river, shops and small stone houses lined the narrow streets.

▲ The lower town in Québec was home to carpenters, such as these oarmakers.

The Acadians

Although the French had abandoned their settlement at Port Royal in 1607, a small farming community gradually grew up on the same site. By the mid-1700s, Acadia was home to over 14,000 settlers.

In the 1630s, small groups of French immigrants settled around the trading posts on the Bay of Fundy. Instead of clearing the forests for their farms, they built **dikes** on the tidal flats to keep out the sea. In these fertile marshlands, they grew wheat and other crops and raised their animals.

Acadia did not have only French settlements. The English had been active in the area since the early 1600s. As a result of wars between France and England in Europe and in North America, Acadia was sometimes controlled by the French and sometimes by the English. In the 100 years between 1613 and 1713, the colony changed hands nine times. In 1713, Acadia finally became an English territory.

At first, little changed for the Acadians, but in 1755, the English governor demanded that the Acadians swear an **oath of allegiance** to the King of England. Most refused to take the oath. An order went out that all land and animals belonging to the Acadians were to be **confiscated**. The Acadians were rounded up and loaded onto transport ships, taking with them only what they could carry.

▲ **The English forced the Acadians to leave behind their land, their homes, and most of their possessions.**

A Peaceful People

When the Acadians were asked to swear allegiance to the King of England, they were willing to **compromise**. They refused to promise to fight on the English side in a war with France, but they agreed to remain **neutral**. This arrangement did not satisfy the English governor of the colony. Because he wanted the Acadians to promise to be loyal to the British, he deported three-quarters of the Acadian population. The U.S. poet Henry Wadsworth Longfellow commemorated this tragic event in his poem "Evangeline," a story of a young Acadian girl and her lover who were separated, **exiled** from their homeland, and only reunited at the end of their lives.

▶ A statue of Evangeline in St. Martinville, Louisiana.

EVANGELINE

Ten thousand Acadians were forced to leave their homes. Families were split up, herded onto ships, and deported to France, other French colonies, or to the English colonies along the Atlantic coast, where many were kept in prisoner-of-war camps. Other Acadians escaped north into the woods or made the long journey south to the French colony of Louisiana, where their **descendants** live today. The English then burned the Acadian villages to the ground.

▼ A village in Louisiana where Acadians settled after they were forced to leave their homes in the mid-1700s.

The deportation continued for eight years. Finally, in 1763, because they were no longer considered a threat by the English, 1000 Acadians returned to Acadia. They found that their farmland had been taken over by English settlers. The Acadians made their way into what is today the province of New Brunswick where they tried to start a new life.

End of New France

In the 1700s, France and England were often at war with each other. The conflict between these two powerful countries spilled over into North America. In 1763, France lost all its North American colonies.

From the earliest days of New France, the French and the English had fought over their colonies in North America. In 1629, the English captured Québec. Although it was returned to the French in 1632, this event was a taste of things to come.

After the French king took over control of New France in 1663, the colony began to expand west and south. The French wanted to increase the fur trade and control a port that was not blocked by ice for many months of the year. French explorers traveled into the Ohio and Mississippi River valleys, building a series of fur-trading forts along the way. In 1669, they founded the French colony of Louisiana, named after the French king Louis. The English colonies felt threatened by this expansion, and a series of minor battles resulted.

In 1744, England and France were at war again in Europe. The conflict spread to North America, and both countries sent large armies with trained commanders to their colonies. The English captured French forts along the Ohio and advanced north to Québec.

▶ A drummer takes part in a reenactment, in which people act out an event in history, such as a battle. Here, the soldiers are reenacting events that led to the end of French rule in North America.

The Plains of Abraham

The historic battle that ended French control in North America began on the night of September 13, 1759. French troops, under the leadership of the Marquis de Montcalm, had gathered in Québec. The English general James Wolfe decided to launch a surprise attack. In the middle of the night, he led his army of 4300 men up the 180-foot (60-meter) cliffs to a farmer's field known as the Plains of Abraham. In the morning, Montcalm and his soldiers came out to meet them. In fifteen minutes, the battle was over. Wolfe was dead; Montcalm was wounded and died the next day. The English took control of the town of Québec.

▲ The Marquis de Montcalm died of his battle wounds.

▼ Wolfe led his soldiers up the steep cliffs along the St. Lawrence and attacked the French.

Québec was not only the center of government in New France, it was the symbol of French control in North America. Its capture by English troops would mean French defeat. France sent extra soldiers, but they were stopped by the British navy.

In a decisive battle at Québec in 1759, the English overwhelmed the French on the Plains of Abraham. After the English took Québec, the French retreated to Montréal where they were again defeated by the English. On September 8, 1760, the French governor surrendered to the English. This event marked the end of New France and all French control in North America.

The future of the French colonists seemed uncertain under English control. However, for 240 years, the French **culture**, language, traditions, and religion have survived. The former glory of New France and the English conquest have never been forgotten. Today, license plates in the province of Québec, carry the words, *"Je me souviens,"* which means, "I remember."

Francophone Culture Today

There are over six million descendants of the early French settlers in Canada. Five million live in the province of Québec. The rest are scattered across Canada from the Atlantic provinces to British Columbia.

Culture is the way people in a community live. It includes their language and religion, their food and music. Art, literature, and architecture are all part of people's culture. **Minorities** in both the United States and Canada, the descendants of the French immigrants have struggled to keep alive their traditions and culture in the face of great odds.

French-speaking people in Canada are called francophones. In the United States, they are called Franco-Americans. During the mid-nineteenth century, almost a million people from poor farming areas in the province of Québec moved to the United States. They settled mostly in the New England states, where they found work in factories. Over the years, most of these Franco-Americans became English speaking. Today, many are rediscovering their French **heritage.**

In Canada, many French speakers are **bilingual**, but some speak only French. Formal French is close to the French spoken in France today. Some francophones use a **dialect** known as *joual*. *Joual* mixes French with English and Native-American words.

▼ **Michel Tremblay's play *The Sisters-in-Law* celebrates *joual*, a dialect of Québec.**

V theatre du rideau vert
direction: yvette brind'amour, mercedes palomino

les belles soeurs
de michel tremblay
mise en scène: andré brassard

revue théâtre, vol. 11, no 7, 20 mai 1971

▲ *Sous le vent de l'île* (*Leeward of the Island*), Paul-Emile Borduas's 1947 painting.

By the 1960s, many francophones realized that Québec was still living in the past. They demanded changes in the role of the Roman Catholic Church, better schools, and improved job opportunities. As more francophones went to university and technical schools, they welcomed the challenges of modern society. In addition, the Québecois birthrate, once the highest in the country, was soon the lowest. These changes sparked a debate about the future of French culture in Québec.

Authors and artists were some of the first to express the need for change. One of the first artists who worked to create a new society was Paul-Emile Borduas. He wanted complete freedom of expression for all Québeckers. He felt the church and the government prevented them from having this freedom. Many people were shocked by his opinions, which he wrote in a book called *Refus global*. Borduas was fired from his teaching job, and he moved to France. Borduas's book, and others like it, marked the beginnings of a cultural change in Québec that was later called the Quiet Revolution.

Since the 1960s, many writers, musicians, playwrights, and poets have written about the changes in Québec society. Some are **separatists**, who feel that the French language and culture in Québec make the province different from the rest of Canada. They want Québec to form an independent country.

▼ Québeckers gather together to show their support for Québec's separating from the rest of Canada.

The Cajun Lifestyle

The Acadians in Louisiana established a unique lifestyle that is an important part of that state's culture to this day. Many of them settled in New Orleans, where they became known as the Cajuns.

The word "Cajun" is thought to come from "Acadian" or "Canadian." The name was given to those French settlers who were driven out of Acadia by the British in the eighteenth century and went to southern Louisiana. Today, the Cajuns live in small communities in that part of the state, known as French Louisiana, and also in parts of Texas. Most of them farm cattle and grow crops such as corn, sugar cane, cotton, and yams. They speak a French that combines English, Spanish, German, and Native American languages.

Cajun often lived in **isolated** communities. Because Cajuns kept to themselves, their culture remained unchanged for so long. Sometimes, they were **persecuted** by non-Cajun Americans who often were suspicious of them and disapproved of their "foreign" ways. In the early 1900s, an attempt was made to force them to give up their culture. Cajun children were forbidden to speak the language of their ancestors in schools.

▲ Bayous, Cajun for "rivers," especially slow ones, are sung about in many Cajun songs.

A Cajun Classic

Andouille, a thick Cajun sausage, is a great favorite in New Orleans. It is made with lean pork and pork fat, with a lot of garlic. The sausage is also used in an oyster and andouille gumbo, which was made popular in Laplace, a Cajun town close to New Orleans. Laplace, which means "the place" in French, calls itself the "Andouille Capital of the World." Along with poultry, fish, and seafood such as oysters and shrimp, alligator is an important ingredient in some Cajun recipes.

▼ Cajun chef Paul Prudhomme shows off his jambalaya, a rice and meat stew.

▲ Ironwork balconies decorate many of the older houses in New Orleans.

Although the Cajuns have now been exposed to modern U.S. culture, many of them have been able to keep some of their old ways. Today, they are known for their folk music and their unique style of cooking, which includes ingredients such as pigeon peas, spices, and rich sauces, and specializes in dishes such as jambalayas, gumbos, and blackened catfish.

The music of the Cajuns is usually a song, sung to the accompaniment of a fiddle or an accordion and other instruments. The rhythm may be slow and dreamy, like a waltz, or fast and upbeat. It is not just for listening but is played at dances, which the Cajuns call *fais do do*. Through the years, Cajun music has been influenced by other musical forms, including jazz, blues, and country and western. Recently, traditional Cajun music has made a comeback. It is played on the radio and is featured at music festivals. Many of the songs date back to the music that the original settlers of Acadia and Québec brought with them from France so long ago.

Here to Stay

The French communities in Canada and the United States have produced many people who have made important political, scientific, and artistic contributions to North American life.

Some of Canada's greatest political leaders have come from Québec. Sir Wilfred Laurier, one of the country's most respected leaders, was the country's first francophone prime minister. Pierre Elliott Trudeau was Canada's most high-profile prime minister. He was head of the government between 1968 and 1983.

All over the world, the name Bombardier is known in the field of transportation. Joseph-Armand Bombardier was an inventor. In the 1920s, the roads of rural Québec were covered with deep snow in winter, making it difficult for a car or even a horse-drawn sleigh to get through. Bombardier invented a motorized sled he called the Ski-Doo. Today, the Bombardier company is a leader in the manufacture of aerospace, transportation, and rail products.

▲ Geneviève Bujold, from Montréal, has had a long international career. She has starred in many movies, including *Anne of a Thousand Days* and *Murder by Decree*.

◄ Francophone Jacques Villeneuve, a Formula-1 car driver, is Canada's most famous racing driver.

Circus Act

The world-famous, Québec-based circus, Cirque du Soleil, started off as a group of street performers in 1980. Today, its dazzling shows mix high-wire acts, contortionists, jugglers, stilt-walkers, and clowns with fabulous costumes, original lighting, and unique music. The group, whose name means circus of the sun, has toured all over Canada, the United States, and Europe. It performed before an audience of millions at the televised Atlanta Olympic Games in 1996. Cirque du Soleil has a permanent "big top" in Montréal, Québec, and a year-round troupe in Las Vegas, Nevada.

▶ **The Cirque du Soleil features only human performers in very imaginative costumes and roles and has no animal acts.**

In the arts, francophone musicians, poets, film makers, and actors are known around the world. In the 1950s and 1960s, Québec musicians created a musical style different from most popular English and U.S. music. They sang about Québec's cultural and political issues in a style of folk music. The best known of those **chansonniers** was Gilles Vigneault. His song, "*Mon Pays*" ("My Country") became an unofficial Québec anthem. Today, the singer Céline Dion has sold millions of albums and is popular among both French- and English-speaking audiences. Many Cajuns have also made their mark in the field of music, including fiddle player Luderin Darbonne.

Québec film makers have won prizes around the world for their work. The director Claude Jutra is best known for his movie *Mon oncle Antoine*, one of the most popular films made in Canada. It is the story of a young boy, set in the past in a small town on Christmas eve.

Julie Payette is a Canadian Space Agency astronaut. She completed her first mission in May 1999. Julie is an athlete as well as a scientist.

▼ **Astronaut Julie Payette performs experiments in a space station.**

Glossary

ancestor Family member from the past, such as a great-grandparent.

baptism A ceremony involving water that makes someone a member of the Christian Church.

bilingual Someone who can speak two languages.

chapel A small Christian church.

chansonnier A writer and singer of music-hall songs and cabaret songs.

Christianity The religion of those who follow the teachings of Jesus Christ and the Bible.

colony Area of land settled or conquered by a distant state and controlled by it.

compromise Agreement reached by two sides who have different points of view.

confiscate To take away, especially by someone in a position of authority.

convert To change from one religion to another.

cultivate To prepare land to grow food plants or other plants in it.

culture A group of people's way of life, including their language, beliefs, and art.

descendant A family member such as a child, a grandchild, and their children.

dialect A form of language used by people living in a particular district.

dowry The money or valuable objects a woman brings to her marriage, usually paid by her parents.

dike An earth wall.

emigration When someone leaves their country to make their home in another.

epidemic A time when many people have the same sickness.

exclusive For the use of one group of people only.

excommunication Taking away someone's membership in the Christian Church.

exile To be sent away from one's own country.

fabled Much talked about.

foreigner Someone from another country.

heritage The language, beliefs, lifestyles, and art that people receive from previous generations.

import Bring objects to one country from another country.

insulator A material that can keep the heat in.

isolated Away from other people.

minority A small number.

missionaries Religious people who work to change other people's religious beliefs to their own.

monopoly Complete control over something that is produced and sold.

morale General mood.

neutral Not taking sides.

oath of allegiance Promise made to an authority to be on their side.

persecute To treat badly.

separatist A group of people who want to separate out from another group of people.

trek A long journey.

Index

1 2 3 4 5 6 7 8 9 0 Printed in the USA 5 4 3 2 1 0